Hurst Castle

HAMPSHIRE

J G COAD MA, FSA

Inspector of Ancient Monuments and Historic Buildings

Hurst Castle, low and menacing on its shingle spit, is the most powerful of the defences established since the sixteenth century to guard the western entrance to the Solent. The Tudor castle, built between 1541 and 1544, was extensively modernised during the Napoleonic wars. Its defences were updated again in the 1850s and most spectacularly in the 1860s and 1870s by the addition of the two massive casemated wings which dominate their surroundings. The castle was garrisoned in both world wars.

Visitors today can see the Tudor castle, where there is an exhibition in the north-west bastion on the defences of this area, and parts of the Victorian west wing. The Victorian east wing is not open but can be viewed from the top of the Tudor castle. *A chronological tour begins on page 3.*

ENGLISH HERITAGE · LONDON

CONTENTS

Published by English Heritage
23 Savile Row, London W1S 2ET
© *Copyright English Heritage 1985*
First published 1985
Second edition 1990, reprinted 1991, 1995, 1997, 2000, 2001, 2003
Printed in England by Matthews the Printers Ltd, London E4
0563, 38776, 05739, 03/03, C30
ISBN 1 85074 053 4

DESCRIPTION AND TOUR

Hurst Castle from the south east. In the centre is the much altered outline of Henry VIII's castle, on either side the massive wing batteries begun in 1861

The full majesty of Hurst Castle is best viewed from the sea, but most visitors will approach it from the rear or landward side. Although Henry VIII's castle was sited here to guard the Solent entrance, it was designed to withstand assaults from both sea and land and its armament was disposed symmetrically round it, as can be seen in the embrasures (*see Glossary*) and gun loops of the Tudor north-west bastion. By contrast, the Victorian military engineers of the 1860s were not so concerned with a serious landward assault. Their wings present formidable but largely blank façades to the mainland although provision was made at the end of the west wing for guns to cover the approach along the spit. The two Victorian entrances were protected by limited secondary armament mounted in the Tudor west bastion and by rifle fire from the small brick covered passage or caponier of 1852 in what remained of the Tudor moat.

This is one suggested itinerary, visiting the castle in a chronological order. The present entrance to the castle is through the **gateway** dated 1873 into the west wing. The former guard room, opening off the entrance passage, contains part of the mechanism which once operated the lifting bridge.

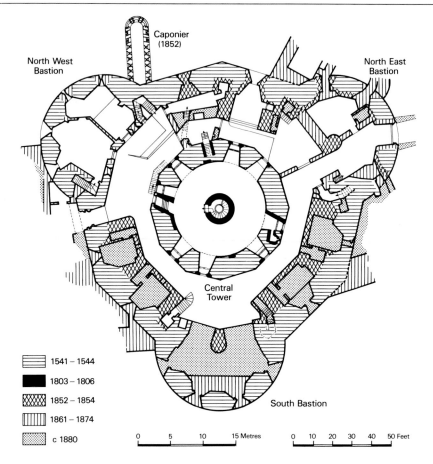

Key:
- ▤ 1541 – 1544
- ■ 1803 – 1806
- ▨ 1852 – 1854
- ▥ 1861 – 1874
- ▧ c 1880

The ground floor of Hurst Castle (detail)

The Tudor castle

Inside the entrance the west wing, built in the 1860s, can be seen stretching away to the right; to the left is the Tudor castle. Over the entrance gateway to the latter is a blank plaque supported by two shallow columns or pilasters, very similar to one in the corresponding position at Calshot Castle. These plaques probably once contained the royal coats-of-arms.

On either side of the plaque are circular holes for drawbridge chains, a reminder that the moat once surrounded the castle

and survived here until 1861.

Inside the vaulted gateway in front of the double doors are slots for the portcullis or defensive grille. Immediately beyond it is the central tower.

The central tower

The central tower, circular within, is twelve sided externally. It has two floors and a basement. Over the doorway to the ground floor is the date 1585 and a mason's mark, witness to some late Tudor repairs and refinements. Within, five steps lead up to an inner doorway.

The present floor level dates from the 1803 rebuild of the keep interior. In the 1880s this floor was thickened with approximately 4ft (1.2m) of concrete to give greater protection to the magazine below. This filling has now been removed but its insertion explains the heightening of the fireplaces.

For much of its time, this **ground-floor room** probably provided living quarters for the garrison, its space initially subdivided by timber and wattle partitions. The room is lit by eight windows with pointed heads, arranged symmetrically in pairs in embrasures. These were not primarily for defence as they are below the level of the curtain wall. The windows were altered externally and given square heads in the early nineteenth century. In the 1880s a window on the east side was converted into a doorway to provide an entry for stores.

The small chamber in the wall thickness on the south-east side was once a garderobe or latrine. The room is built round a central brick pier which dates from the 1803 alterations; this contains a staircase down to the lighting chamber which lit the magazine. The present small iron door dates from the 1880s when it replaced a much larger door. As first built in 1541–44, central spiral stairs led from the basement to the roof.

The **first floor** is now reached by external stairs probably constructed in the 1880s, which leads to a former window. The room's internal arrangements were probably much the same in Tudor times and like the floor below once provided various rooms for accommodation for the garrison. The eight windows look out above the level of the curtain walls and hand weapons or small carriage-mounted pieces could have been fired through them. As below, four fireplaces warmed this floor. The fine brick vaulting dates from 1803–06. There are three small

The entrance to the Tudor castle. The moat here was infilled in 1861

lobbies in the thickness of the wall. That to the west formed an entrance to a door, now blocked, immediately above a ground-floor door. Just within the entrance to the chamber to the north east is an original blocked doorway in the external wall, whilst the window in the small room on the south side replaces a doorway here. All three doorways once led to timber bridges across to the bastions. Beyond the north-east lobby is a garderobe.

The **roof** is reached by the staircase inside the central pier. The cupboard near the top was inserted in 1853 to contain four boxes or 44 rounds of ready-use ammunition for the guns on the roof. The brackets above were for six rammers, six sponges and six wadhooks for the 32 pdr guns. The roof and parapets were much altered in nineteenth century; the latter once had rounded battlements similar to those of the north-west bastion. The grand central

The central tower. The blocked doorway once led to a walkway connecting with the north-west bastion (see opposite)

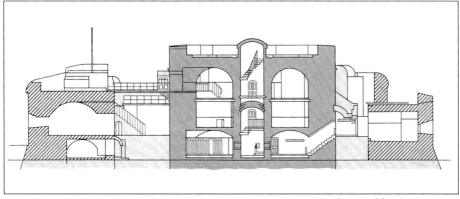

Cross-section of Hurst Castle, c1870, showing the walkways connecting keep and bastions

cupola or dome was superseded in 1805 by a glazed lantern, in turn replaced by the existing more functional and less vulnerable one in the 1850s. The remains of the gun mountings date from the early 1850s when heavier ordnance replaced four 32 pdr traversing guns covering the sea passage and two on swivels on the north side of the roof.

From the roof are superb views of the Hampshire coast and the Isle of Wight. Across the Needles Passage is the squat brick Fort Albert with its three tiers of gun ports, begun in 1854, while the silhouette of Needles Battery [National Trust] can be seen on the cliffs above the Needles. Less visible fortifications on the Isle of Wight stand witness to the importance of protecting this sea passage to the commercial port of Southampton and the naval base at Portsmouth.

Originally, the central tower and courtyard were surrounded by a curtain wall with three semi-circular bastions projecting to the north-east, north-west and south. All were extensively altered in the nineteenth century and only the north-west bastion retains most of its original form.

The north-west bastion

Probably because it covered the landward approach and the gateway, the north-west bastion was the most powerful of the three with a basement, two floors and a flat roof for a further tier of guns. The **ground-floor room**, originally a single large chamber, had four gun ports for the main armament. The southernmost embrasure is masked by the 1860s west wing. Its neighbour was adapted at this time to take a 64 pdr RML on a traversing carriage which covered the entrance to the west wing, while the remaining two embrasures were narrowed to form rifle loops, new stonework being carefully inserted into the face of the bastion wall. The northernmost embrasure still has its Tudor smoke vent, a reminder of the huge clouds of smoke generated by exploding gunpowder. The brick partition wall dates from the 1860s when part of this floor was converted into ablutions for the garrison. The two blocked Tudor windows which once lit the room can be seen from the courtyard.

To the right of the bastion a doorway opens to narrow stairs to the first floor and the roof. Like the ground floor, the **first floor** was designed to carry guns as well as provide living accommodation for some of the garrison. Four fireplaces once warmed it, that in the side of the northern embrasure also containing a bread oven. In the south-east wall is a garderobe, later altered to a cupboard. The southern of the two gun embrasures was blocked by construction of the west wing; possibly at the same time the adjacent window was inserted. The two windows overlooking the courtyard have had their side walls or splays altered in the nineteenth century. This room now contains an exhibition about the castle.

Next to the former garderobe, a doorway leads to the **portcullis chamber** over the main gateway. Here can be seen the portcullis complete with its weights and chains. Although the castle had provision for a portcullis from the beginning, this one is not the original, while its housing probably dates mostly from the early 1850s.

Adjacent to the portcullis room are stairs which once led to the **roof**. The top is now blocked and access is by the stair on the north side of the bastion. The flat roof, which is a modern replacement, was originally designed to carry a third tier of guns firing through five embrasures.

The rear of the north-west bastion from the keep

The central tower and north-west bastion of the Tudor castle, seen from the former moat. On the right is the northern caponier begun in 1852, and the only one to survive the great modernisation started in 1861 (Photo: J G Coad)

From the roof is a fine view of the west wing and beyond it the shingle spit linking with the mainland.

When returning down the stairs, note the blocked doorway which once gave access to the Tudor wall walk. Back in the courtyard, the adjacent Tudor doorway leads down to the basement of the north-west bastion. This was fitted with water tanks in the latter half of the nineteenth century and is not open to visitors. However, at the bottom of the steps a short passage leads into a **caponier**. This is the only survivor of three built in 1852, their rifle loops effectively covering all the immediate approaches to the castle. In Tudor times, two gun embrasures at basement level in the bastions fulfilled much the same function. The one visible at the front of the stairs was probably blocked when the

caponier was built, while its companion was hidden when the moat was partly infilled at a later date.

The north curtain

The brick wall connecting the north-east corner of the north-west bastion with the keep forms part of the 1860s alterations. A doorway at its northern end leads to the rear of the Tudor north curtain wall which was extensively reformed in the early 1850s. Originally, there were two gun embrasures in the curtain walls between each bastion. The wooden steps, which replace a concrete ramp, lead to a well-protected chamber at the top of the cartridge hoist from the keep basement. Hoist and chamber probably date from the late 1870s, but for long before then, the basement had been used as a gunpowder store. Opposite the cartridge hoist an early nineteenth-century doorway leads down to the Tudor basement.

The basement

The basement is a circular room with recesses in the walls for stacking powder barrels and then shells. The central brick pier supporting the vault has a partly defaced inscription running round the top recording that the keep was repaired and reformed in 1805, the date of the pier and vaulting. The pier contains a staircase to the ground floor as well as lamp chambers enabling the magazine or ammunition store to be lit without the danger of taking lamps directly into it.

To increase safety, the late 1870s alterations blocked the doorway at the bottom of the stair and inserted additional lamp recesses here. At this time the basement held 1100 12-inch cartridges and 1150 10-inch cartridges together with sufficient gunpowder to fill them, less than a third of the total heavy ammunition then in the fortress. Earlier generations, less safety-conscious, used the basement for a variety of purposes. During the Napoleonic wars, food, fuel and general stores were kept here as well as gunpowder. A number of replica powder barrels can be seen.

The north-east bastion

On leaving the basement turn right and go down the concrete slope. Opposite, the substantial brick wall linking the keep to the north-east bastion was built in the 1860s to give a measure of protection here from enfilading fire, that is, enemy fire sweeping the whole length of the castle. On the left is a brick casemate containing the rails for a traversing carriage for a 64 pdr RML gun. This casemate forms part of the 1852 improvements and adapted one of the Tudor emplacements.

A stairway adjacent to the rear of the Tudor north-east bastion leads to the roof. The Tudor north-east and south bastions each had a basement, ground floor and flat roof enabling two tiers of guns to be mounted. Both were extensively modified in the nineteenth century and it is now possible to visit only part of the roof.

The roof of the north-east bastion was reformed at the beginning of the nineteenth century to take three traversing carriages, probably armed with captured French 8pdrs known to have been here in 1804. In the early 1850s, both this and the south bastion were extensively altered by insertion of the existing casemates enabling the mounting of far heavier weapons – 8-inch shell guns on dwarf traversing carriages and 32 pdr guns. The brick and stone recesses for ammunition behind the parapets belong to this phase.

The north-east bastion was masked by construction of the east wing in the 1860s when an entrance to the latter was cut through the bastion and the remaining parts of the ground floor and basement were adapted as shell stores.

The south bastion

From the north-east bastion, steps lead down to the curtain wall linking with the south bastion. This curtain too was extensively modified in the early 1850s to incorporate two casemates at ground level; only the outer wall retains its Henrician form and materials. By the 1880s this seaward side of the Tudor castle was considered too vulnerable to new naval weapons and to protect the magazine in the keep basement the curtain casemates along with most of the interior of the south bastion were filled with concrete and shingle. As part of the same precautions, the south half of the courtyard had 7 ft (2.1 m) of concrete laid on it; this was removed in the 1970s.

The Tudor south bastion has been extensively masked by later alterations and additions and its form is best seen from the beach. After modifications in the 1860s, its roof carried two 64 pdr RML guns. Two short wing walls, with rifle loops protecting the steps to the roof and the guns' crews, remain from this period; the present massive concrete gun emplacement was added at the beginning of this century. Beyond, the curtain linking with the Tudor north-west bastion was modified for two casemated guns in the early 1850s, but these were masked by construction of the west wing some ten years later and further hidden by construction of a gun battery at the beginning of this century.

From the roof of the south bastion retrace your route to the entrance to the Tudor castle to visit the 1860s west wing.

The courtyard of the 1860s east wing can be visited by going through the entrance cut through the north-east bastion. Unlike its western counterpart, this never had emplacements for modern armament added, and it remains little altered since completion. On its roof near the centre is one of the original and very exposed fire-control positions. To the rear, the two massive grass-covered structures are the main magazines for this part of the fortress.

The 1860s west wing

The 1860s extensions to Hurst Castle in the form of two massive wing batteries were designed to house a total of 30 heavy guns of varying calibres all concentrating on hostile warships attempting the Needles Passage. If so vast an armament seems excessive, it must be remembered that such weapons took some time to reload and the

Entrance to the west wing with its original drawbridge

casemates – necessary to protect them and their detachments – restricted their angles of fire. Steam-driven warships entering service in the 1860s were steadily increasing in speed and it is more than probable that each heavy gun at Hurst would have only one opportunity to fire at a particular target. If a hostile fleet forced the Needles Passage, there was little between it and Southampton, and little to stop it disembarking an army on the Gosport Peninsula and threatening the western approaches to Portsmouth Dockyard. Thus there were very cogent arguments for the safety in numbers approach at Hurst.

The west wing in 1886 held a total of ten 12.5-inch 38-ton guns and five 10-inch 18-ton guns along with one 64 pdr for more local defence. All guns and their detachments were protected by

Top: The front of one of the casemates at Hurst, showing its massive iron shield which was evolved as a result of the Shoeburyness experiments (see page 27). Below: A woven rope mantlet photographed in an experimental casemate at Shoeburyness in the late 1860s

massive granite-fronted casemates given extra security by the addition of immensely thick wrought-iron shields in front of the guns. In the floors can be seen the iron racers and the toothed traversing racks for the gun carriages.

In the casemates adjacent to the entrance to the Tudor castle are two 12.5-inch guns. The barrels were salvaged from the Isle of Wight and the traversing carriages are modern simplified replicas.

The awesome size and cumbersome nature of these huge weapons can be easily appreciated. Each needed twelve men to operate it. Adjacent to the gun are modern replicas of the cast-iron shells. These weighed over 800 lb; propelled by a charge of $43\frac{1}{2}$ lb of cordite, they could be fired some 6000 yards. Forward of the muzzle is a replica shell lift.

Immediately to the rear of the armoured iron shield which forms the front of the casemate hangs a woven rope mantlet. Such mantlets were designed to absorb lethal splinters from the shields if the latter sustained direct hits, and to help keep out some of the vast quantities of smoke produced by firing the gun. (Within the brick vault here and in the other casemates can be seen flues also designed to channel away the gun smoke.) When the fortress went into action, the mantlets were wetted with a solution of calcium chloride and water to prevent them being ignited by gunfire. This mantlet is a modern replica.

The rear of each casemate was designed as living accommodation for the garrison and originally was enclosed by timber and glass screens which would be dismantled before action. A few of these screens survive intact, but most were modified during the 1914-18 and 1939-45 wars. Over the years, the army adapted casemates into a variety of uses. Towards the western end of the west wing one was turned into the garrison theatre

Right: These two photographs of the late 1860s show one of the new muzzle-loading weapons of the kind used at Hurst. The first shows a 13.3-inch RML in its casemate, with rammer and mop to the rear, and a shell and its charge in the foreground. The second picture shows the method of loading the shell into the barrel

during the 1939-45 war. This retains part of its wartime scenery and also houses rare twin 6 pdr guns with King Edward VIII's cypher on them. These once formed part of the castle's armament. Nearer to the guard room there survives an earlier ablution room with its rows of basins. This latter probably dates from the time of the garrison latrines which remain in use below the iron lighthouse. Projecting into the courtyard between groups of casemates are magazines, their contents protected in secure storage below ground level. The flower beds are a recreation of the 1939-45 garrison garden.

The west wing has two well-projected main magazines to the rear, one just outside the entrance of the Tudor castle, the other at the western extremity of the wing. When construction started in 1861, foundations for casemates for troops' accommodation were put in along the inside of the rear wall. These were not built, but their blocked fireplace openings are still visible.

West of the main entrance is a series of single-storey brick buildings constructed as detention cells, canteen, coal and artillery stores. Built into the rear wall here is the 1865 lighthouse; Trinity House asserted their independence of the fortress by insisting on direct access to this from outside. Their doorway still survives surmounted by their coat-of-arms. This lighthouse was superseded by the adjacent iron light built in 1911; still in use, it is unusual in that it is gas lit. The 1880s narrow-gauge railway was used to shift stores and ammunition from the pier.

The brick and concrete emplacements on the roof of the west wing were added at the beginning of this century and modified and extended in 1914-18 and 1939-45. They originally contained searchlights, look-out and fire-control positions and 12 pdr quick-firing guns.

These last weapons, supplementing a battery of three lighter weapons east of the east wing, by their speed of fire and accuracy superseded the vast casemated guns below them, although some of the latter remained in reserve here as late as 1918. Projecting on to the sea shore in front of the west wing are two concrete searchlight emplacements which date from c1900. Hurst Castle retained armament until the abolition of the coastal artillery arm of the British army in 1956.

Outside the fortress are remains of other gun emplacements. A little to the west are the eroded earthworks of the West Battery of 1852, the tumbled vestiges of some of the expense magazines on the shore witness to the unceasing assaults of the sea here. At the east end of the east wing are concrete emplacements for three 6 pdr quick-firing guns which were added in 1893 specifically to counter the fast torpedo boats then coming into service with naval powers. Ammunition for these guns was passed through a hatch, now blocked, cut into the end of the east wing.

Today, the permanent population of the shingle spit is probably the smallest since work began on the castle in 1541. The scatter of existing houses was mostly built for lighthouse keepers and coastguards. Outside the castle the most prominent structure is the **lighthouse,** begun in 1865 and completed in 1867. The first lighthouse here lay a little to the west of the castle and was begun in 1786. To aid navigators it was supplemented by a second, taller lighthouse begun in 1812. This was called the High Light and its predecessor renamed the Low Light. The latter stood in the way of the west wing of the castle and was replaced by a new Low Light built on to the rear wall of the west wing. The High Light of 1812 lay some 50ft (15.2m) west of its 1867 successor.

HISTORY

Hurst Castle on its shingle spit (a 1954 photograph: Aerofilms)

The long shingle spit which curves out from the Hampshire coast at Milford on Sea towards the Isle of Wight narrows the western entrance of the Solent to some 1400 yards (1280 m). Through this entrance the ebb and flow of the tides create strong currents which can still halt vessels attempting the passage against them. Apart from stationing a naval force in the area, before the sixteenth century there was no way of denying the channels through this entrance to hostile ships. By the early 1500s though, advances in the new science of artillery meant that in theory this gap could be commanded by guns mounted on shore. Defence here was highly desirable, for this was one of the two sea routes to the great commercial port of Southampton with its rich and vulnerable hinterland, to the

heart of the Isle of Wight and to Portsmouth, then beginning its slow rise to prominence as a naval arsenal.

The first recorded attempt to control this passage was the construction of a gun tower by Sir James Worsley, Governor of the Isle of Wight. Worsley's Tower, as it was known, was a small octagonal structure built on the foreshore of the island opposite the site of the future Hurst Castle. It was probably constructed in the 1520s and may have had provision for heavy guns on its roof. In concept it was similar to the still-surviving but earlier gun towers at the entrance to Portsmouth Harbour and in the centre of Camber Castle in Sussex. Worsley's Tower, however, had two serious weaknesses: its small size limited the number of weapons it could hold,

15

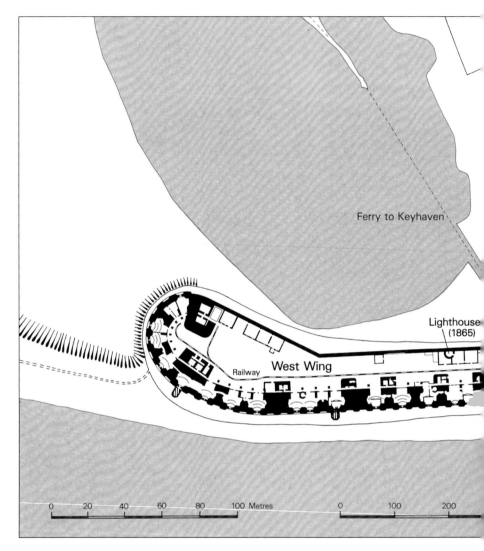

Ferry to Keyhaven

Lighthouse (1865)

Railway West Wing

0 20 40 60 80 100 Metres

0 100 200

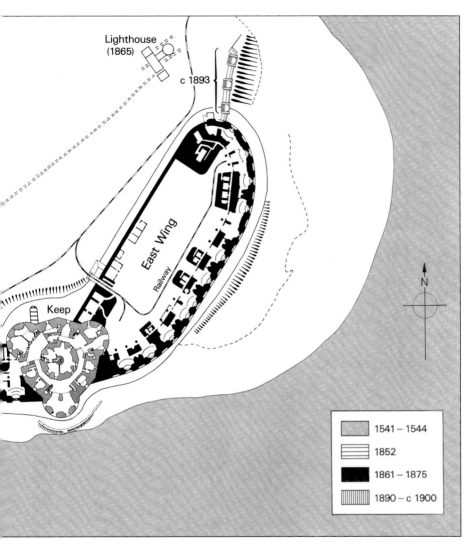

Lighthouse
(1865)

c 1893

East Wing

Railway

Keep

N

1541 – 1544

1852

1861 – 1875

1890 – c 1900

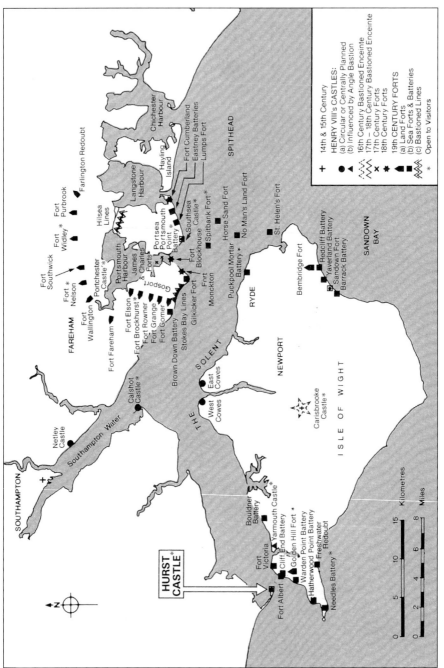

Defences of the Solent area

while its position at the foot of the cliffs made it particularly vulnerable to a raiding party approaching it overland.

In the deteriorating political climate of the late 1530s, Worsley's Tower was rightly considered inadequate to its task. Henry VIII's break with the Roman Catholic Church, together with the offence caused to the Emperor Charles V by the annulment of the king's marriage to his aunt, Catherine of Aragon in 1533, had not posed a real threat to England as long as the principal Catholic military powers in Europe were openly hostile to each other. But in June 1538 Francis I of France and the Emperor Charles V signed a peace treaty almost coincident with the papal Bull excommunicating Henry VIII. Suddenly, invasion of England was felt to be a distinct probability.

Preparations to counter invasion began in earnest early in 1539. Musters of able-bodied men were held, the small fleet was readied, weapons and mercenaries were sought in Antwerp and Hamburg and the warning chain of beacons around the coast was put in order and manned. More significantly, in February 1539 Henry ordered specially appointed commissioners to survey the coasts of England to select sites for defence works to protect likely invasion points, dockyards, fleet anchorages, ports and harbours. The chain of forts from Hull to Milford Haven ultimately built as a result of this survey was the first system of coastal defences since the Roman forts of the Saxon Shore over 1200 years earlier.

The Tudor castle

The two commissioners charged with examining defensive positions around the western part of the Solent, the Earl of Southampton and Lord St John,

recommended the construction of four forts, at Hurst and Calshot on the mainland and East and West Cowes on the Isle of Wight. Construction of the last two was under way by April 1539 but such was the fear of invasion then that temporary earth and timber batteries were built possibly at Calshot and certainly at Hurst pending construction of more durable fortifications.

Before the end of 1539 the likelihood of invasion, perhaps never as great as had been feared, had largely receded. Levies were stood down and the navy reduced, but the king pressed on with his chain of defence works in which he was personally interested and which he undoubtedly saw as a worthwhile investment for the future. Locally, Calshot and East and West Cowes were largely completed by the end of 1540 after which John Mille, the financial controller and his team turned their attention to fortifying the spit at Hurst. Payments for work here began in February 1541 and continued at irregular intervals until January 1544. The castle was sufficiently advanced for a garrison under the captaincy of Thomas Bertie to be established by 1542. Bertie himself, master mason at Calshot and East and West Cowes, was probably also master mason at Hurst. The latter castle and Calshot are unique among Henry VIII's castles in having triangular-headed windows in their central towers.

In design and layout Hurst is one of the most sophisticated of Henry VIII's artillery forts, a reflection perhaps of its late beginning and of the employment of a team already experienced from the. construction of three other forts. The heart of the castle is a twelve-sided tower surrounded by what would have been a geometrically similar curtain wall (*see Glossary*) but for the replacement of alternative pairs of faces by three substantial semi-circular bastions or defensive positions. It was surrounded originally by a moat which survived intact until the early 1850s.

Later alterations have diminished some of the impact of Henry's fortress, but when completed it was extremely powerful. For defence of the immediate area there were six flankers, gun positions designed to fire along the front of the adjacent curtain, at moat level. The main armament was in eighteen casemates or vaulted gun chambers at ground level, eleven embrasures or openings in the curtain parapet, ten in the parapets of the two lower bastions, eight gun ports at the same level in the central tower, and six embrasures in the parapet of the north-west bastion overlooking the entrance. Finally, there were twelve embrasures on the top of the central tower. In all, there were seventy-one gun positions in six tiers. It is highly unlikely that Hurst ever had weapons for each of these, but a 1547 survey indicates that there were around twenty weapons of varying calibre, making Hurst one of the better armed of the coastal forts and a potentially formidable guardian of the Solent passage. Twelve years later, over half this ordnance had been withdrawn but the garrison was still sizeable – a captain and deputy, porter, master gunner, eleven gunners and nine soldiers.

The seventeenth and eighteenth centuries

For the next 250 years there were few alterations of any significance at Hurst but its importance was such that although it suffered periods of neglect it never became wholly ruinous. For most of this time it appears to have had a garrison although the few surviving records suggest that the latter often lacked serviceable weapons and ammunition. In 1628, for example, when ordered to stop

some Flemish ships, the porter had neither powder nor shot and only four or five of the twenty-seven pieces of ordnance were usable.

During the Civil War the castle was occupied by Parliamentary forces and for a brief time in early December 1648 it became a temporary prison for Charles I. He was probably confined in the central tower before being escorted to London to his trial and his execution. In 1650, no doubt influenced by the news that Prince Charles had landed in Jersey, the garrison was increased and powder and shot sent to the castle. After the Restoration, Charles II toyed with demolishing Hurst, but this idea was soon abandoned and between 1673 and

Hurst Castle in the eighteenth century (British Library)

1675 repairs were carried out and a proper garrison re-established.

In 1672 customs officers complained that they were not allowed to search the fortress, which they were told was a centre of smuggling. Its comparatively isolated position, no doubt attractive to smugglers, also made it attractive as a detention centre. In 1700 the Privy Council decided on Hurst Castle as the prison for anyone convicted under the Act for the further preventing the Growth of Popery. In October 1700 a priest named Atkinson was sent here and was to remain a prisoner until his death twenty-nine years later.

Life for the men of the small garrison was isolated but not necessarily lonely, although in the eighteenth century they may well have felt forgotten by their superiors. In Georgian England, postings to garrisons tended to be for long periods – in 1800 the Master Gunner had been here for seventeen years. Such men could have their families living in the castle with them or possibly in accommodation outside. The latter may have been more attractive, for by the mid 1780s long neglect of the fabric had resulted in there being few dry rooms, while lack of equipment must have seriously affected the capabilities of the castle. Guns and mounts were in short supply as were more mundane items – a 1781 report noted that 'gunners have been for a long time obliged to buy brooms to sweep their room and the platforms of the castle.'

But the tedium of garrison life must have been lessened by events around the fortress. Apart from the interest of passing shipping – often within hailing distance – the spit itself was frequented by fishermen who dried their herring catches in timber sheds on the shingle. Construction of the first lighthouse in 1786 added to the permanent population, and plans of the period show gardens on the lee of the shingle bank, their soil carefully collected from neighbouring marshes. An inn – the Shipwright's Arms – stood just outside the castle entrance and was certainly in existence in the 1780s. It continued in business into the

1850s when it had a further brief life as a garrison canteen before being demolished. A successor – the Castle Inn – traded for some years at the north end of the shingle spit beyond the coastguard cottages.

War with France: the castle strengthened

In 1793, the year Britain went to war with Revolutionary France, this strategically important fortress was reported as being in the worst condition of any along this part of the south coast. The following year repairs were authorised and to augment the fire power, two five-gun batteries, armed with

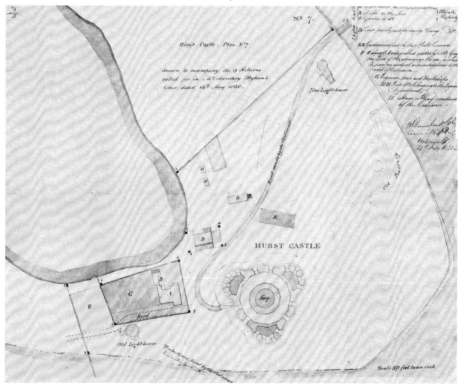

Hurst Castle in 1833. Outside the castle are various dwellings, an inn, gardens and lighthouses. The 'old battery' is one of two authorised in 1794

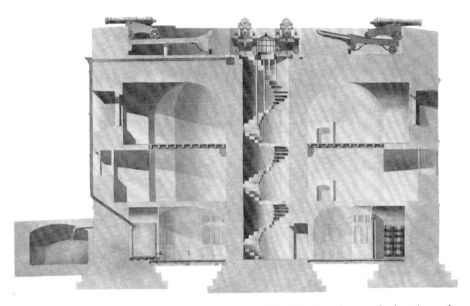

Cross-section of the central tower or keep after the 1803–06 alterations to the interior and insertion of the vaulting

captured French 36 pdr weapons, were established on the beach. The castle itself was equipped with eighteen 9 pdr French guns, then probably the heaviest weapons its fabric could bear, even after repairs. Consideration was also given to establishing three batteries on the Isle of Wight near the site of Worsley's Tower. Hurst Castle entered the nineteenth century in reasonable order but weakly armed by the standards of the day. Heavier armament in the castle would mean expensive strengthening of the Tudor work.

In 1803 war was renewed with France and the country's coastal defences were again brought to a state of readiness. In March the Earl of Chatham, Master of the Ordnance, asked for a report on the possibility of modernising Hurst Castle '... it having been suggested to his lordship that by turning an arch over the top of it, guns might be mounted

thereon.' Responsibility for drawing up the necessary plans lay with Colonel Jonathan Evelegh, senior officer for the Portsmouth district. His proposals, modified by the Board of Ordnance, were the first substantial change to the castle since its completion in 1544, although from the outside it was to appear little different.

Between June 1803 and the end of 1806 the interior of the central tower was gutted and a strong brick vault – the 'arch over the top of it' – inserted to carry six 24 pdr guns on the roof. The basement was likewise vaulted to protect the magazine. In between, the two floors were adapted for garrison accommodation and all levels were linked by a central spiral staircase. On the basement wall of the latter remains part of an inscription recording this work.

Evelegh's proposal for two new batteries outside the castle to replace

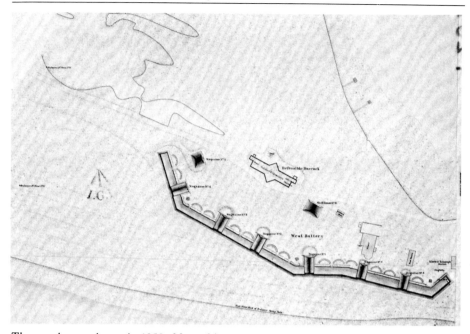

The west battery begun in 1852. Most of it was swept away nine years later, but some of the earthworks and remains of the expense magazines can be seen west of the castle

those constructed some ten years earlier was turned down. Instead, he renewed the timber roofs of the Tudor bastions the better to carry their armament of 8 pdr French guns. All the construction work was carried out by soldiers and workmen – '50 hammocks with bedding' for the latter were sent to Hurst in June 1803. Bricks came from the Board of Ordnance's own brickfields at Stokes Bay on the Gosport Peninsula and from near Fort Cumberland.

All these improvements within the Tudor shell certainly made Hurst a more formidable fortress, but like the great majority of such coastal works, it was not put to the test in this war. Its principal contribution, apart from the deterrence value of its mere existence, was probably as a temporary hospital. On 1 February 1809 all spare space in the castle was appropriated to the Quartermaster-

General's Department for sick and wounded 'now landing with the army arrived from Spain.' As they viewed what at best must have been spartan and draughty quarters in this isolated fortress, one can speculate on the feelings of these men, evacuated across the Bay of Biscay in midwinter by the Royal Navy after an epic 250-mile fighting retreat to Corunna as part of Sir John Moore's army.

Mid nineteenth-century modernisation

For nearly forty years after Evelegh's improvements, little work beyond maintenance was done to Hurst Castle. After 1815 the garrison resumed its leisurely peacetime routine, secure behind the most powerful navy in the world. But by the 1840s this comfortable

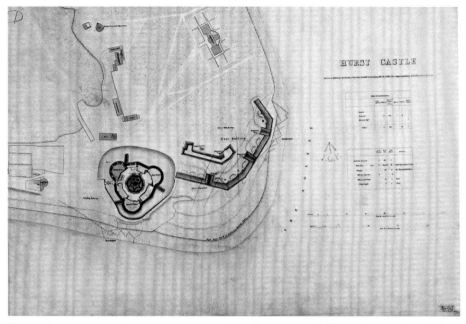

Hurst Castle in 1859. The three caponiers added in 1852 are visible as is the substantial east battery

complacency was being questioned. France was still seen as the natural enemy and it was known that the French were developing new weapons. The introduction of steam-driven merchant vessels and warships made potential invaders largely independent of wind and tide and brought England's vulnerable south coast within a few hours steaming of northern French ports. Coastal defence again became topical and the Board of Ordnance started to spend modest sums on the weakest areas such as the Needles Passage. Two completely new forts were sited on the Isle of Wight: Fort Victoria begun in 1852 and Fort Albert, which still stands complete opposite Hurst Castle, started in 1854. These two powerful works, their design maybe owing something to the earlier Fort Clarence at Chatham, were designed to act in concert with Hurst Castle, which

was undergoing a substantial modernisation at the same time.

In 1850 it was reported that, fully armed, the castle could mount twenty guns: six on the roof of the central tower, four on each of the two seaward bastions and six on the curtain walls. Various proposals to upgrade these and increase their number resulted in work being undertaken in 1851 which probably included repairs to the bastions, the creation of a counterscarp wall round the moat and the deepening of the latter to hold five feet of water. This was probably not completed before another report of December 1851 proposed a more radical and expensive modernisation. In January 1852 the government authorised works totalling some £6725. Over the course of the next four years this sum was probably comfortably exceeded as engineers and contractors modified the castle and built powerful outworks on both sides of it.

Within the castle, the top of the central tower was modified to mount 32 pdr guns and the basement was refloored and equipped to hold 380 powder barrels, sufficient for 100 rounds per gun. The most expensive alterations were reserved for the south and east bastions and curtain walls. Here, massive brick casemates were inserted, allowing for two tiers of heavy weapons. To improve local defence, three covered passages or caponiers, of which one survives, were built in the moat. This work was done by a combination of contractors' workmen and the 7th Company of Royal Sappers and Miners. The latter used the ground floor of the keep as a temporary barracks. Some idea of the conditions here can be gauged by a request in June 1852 for extra fuel to keep the three fires going as even in midsummer the severity of the damp was injuring men's health.

As a result of this work, the old armament of six 24 pdr and fourteen 8 pdr guns was replaced by fifteen 8-inch shell guns, fourteen 32 pdr guns and two 32 pdr carronades.

Outside the castle, two powerful batteries for 8-inch guns were built to the east and west. The former was originally designed for ten guns but in late 1853 two more were added; similarly the west battery, first intended for twelve weapons, ended with seventeen. Behind the latter was built a defensible barracks, sited to form a blockhouse against any raiding party advancing along the shingle spit.

Before all these works were completed, the Crimean War had broken out. Although scenes of fighting in the Black Sea and the Baltic were far removed from Hurst, the profound technical advances in weapons and armaments engendered by the war were to have far-reaching effects on England's coastal defences and were to ensure that the works undertaken in the early 1850s were the shortest lived of all Hurst's modernisations.

In 1859 disquiet among military engineers about the adequacy of Britain's defences coalesced with widespread public alarm that France under the Emperor Napoleon III was preparing an invasion. A Royal Commission was appointed to make recommendations on the defence of the United Kingdom. Its report urged that priority be given to securing the great naval bases against invasion or bombardment by a hostile fleet. Advances in weapons, principally the introduction of the large rifled gun which fired an explosive shell over long distances with great accuracy, meant that new fortifications had to be devised.

In a revised form, the Royal Commission's Report was agreed by the government and Portsmouth, as the country's main naval arsenal, was given priority for a ring of powerful fortresses. An outlying but important element of this scheme was the updating of the defences securing the Needles Passage.

The majority of the works forming the Portsmouth ring defences were land fortresses, facing inland and designed to resist a hostile army which had landed elsewhere. Good examples, which can be visited, are Fort Brockhurst at Gosport and Fort Widley on Portsdown Hill. By contrast, defences at the Needles Passage were designed to sink enemy ships and were not intended to withstand a prolonged overland assault. Here, the aim was to bring the maximum number of heavy guns to bear on the navigable channels. On the Isle of Wight four batteries were established at The Needles, Cliff End, Hatherwood and Warden Point. The garrison for these was based a little inland in a defensible

Two photographs taken in the late 1860s at Shoeburyness Ranges, Essex.
Above: A section of a fort built to find out how well such structures would withstand the impact of the new shells.
Left: The effect of concentrated fire on another section of fortification

barracks of hexagonal shape at Golden Hill. Forts Victoria and Albert were reduced to a secondary role.

At Hurst Castle, the recently completed east and west batteries, formed largely of shingle with earth covering, offered totally inadequate protection to their guns and gunners against the new explosive shells. They were largely demolished and replaced by the present formidable wings. The foundations for these were begun in February 1861 by the Southsea firm of Rogers and Booth. This contract was completed in March 1862 but it was not until May 1863 that the contractors M G Tyrell of Great Yarmouth started work on the superstructures. These were not finished until June 1870 when they still lacked iron shields and the main armament.

Throughout the 1860s, engineers had been experimenting with iron shields on the firing ranges at Shoeburyness in Essex in an effort to produce armoured fronts for the embrasures of forts such as Hurst. Not until the early 1870s did they evolve a reasonably satisfactory design, but such were production problems that the iron shields were probably not completed at Hurst until 1874. The total cost of these immense wings and their associated works came to £211000-17s-9d

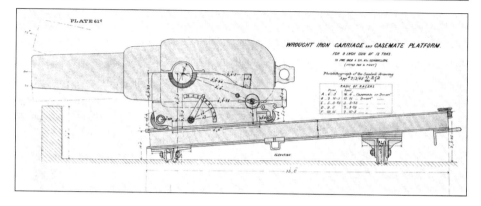

Above: An 1868 drawing of a 9-inch 12-ton RML on its traversing carriage. Left: A photograph taken in the late 1860s showing the method of mounting a 9-inch gun barrel on to its carriage. The massive iron eyes can be seen in the roofs of the vaults at Hurst

of which £79719 was the cost of the iron shields.

In the fifteen years of construction, weapons too had been changing, growing larger and more powerful. When the shields were finally in place, Hurst was armed with a formidable broadside of heavy guns: ten 12.5-inch 38-ton rifled muzzle loaders (RMLs), fifteen 10-inch 18-ton RMLs, five 9-inch 12-ton RMLs and three 64 pdr guns for local defence. In later years, the numbers of these weapons were to vary. There was accommodation, mostly in the rear of the new casemates, for four officers, seven NCOs, and 120 soldiers. The magazine in the basement of the Tudor keep could hold sufficient gunpowder and cartridge

cases for 1100 12-inch shells and 1150 10-inch shells. In addition magazines in the east and west wings held more than twice that amount. The shells themselves were stored in underground shell stores to the rear of the casemates.

But armaments continued to develop. In the 1880s the keep shell store was considered vulnerable to enemy fire and a mass of concrete was added to the ground floor as extra protection. The south bastion was filled solid with shingle and concrete as was much of the south courtyard. By 1890 new and much faster warships were coming into service leading to fears that especially at night, such ships could be safely past Hurst before the ponderous armament could find their range. To counter this threat, by 1893 three 6 pdr quick-firing guns and three 0.45-inch machine guns were added to Hurst's arsenal of weapons. These were mounted in a small open battery in the lee of the east wing of the castle. This battery still exists, its slight design in sharp contrast to the massy fortifications of only thirty years before.

Recent history

Some of the great guns of the 1870s survived at Hurst in working order as secondary armament until after the 1914–18 war, although by then long obsolete. The quick-firing weapons installed in the 1890s had effectively superseded them. These were augmented by a further three 12 pdr quick-firing guns mounted on the tops of the west casemates and on the south bastion early in the new century. Along with these went a pair of searchlights – Defence Electric Lights – which, with others on the Isle of Wight, were to illuminate the Needles Passage at night as part of the counter measures against swift-moving warships.

By then advances in telegraphy and fire-control made Hurst Castle for the first time part of a unified defence system for this area. A Fire Command Post high on the cliffs at new Needles Battery controlled guns there and at Cliff End Battery, Warden Point Battery, Freshwater Redoubt and Hurst Castle.

The castle was garrisoned in both world wars. In the late 1930s some of the weapons were modernised, and the gun positions in the casemate tops were given rudimentary protection against air attack. Hurst was manned in 1941 by the 129 Coastal Battery Royal Artillery. There were two twin 6 pdr quick-firing and two 12 pdr quick-firing guns with searchlights for anti-motor torpedo boat defence. The castle remained an important link in Britain's coastal defences until the abolition in 1956 of the Coastal Artillery Branch of the army.

The War Office gave into care as an ancient monument the Tudor part of the castle in 1933 and the remainder in 1956.

A 38-ton rifled muzzle loader in its casemate at Hurst Castle

In recent years extensive conservation work has been carried out on the keep and Tudor bastions to make them more waterproof and to replace severely eroded or perished stone and brickwork. Work is now being concentrated on rewaterproofing the Victorian west wing and repairing the casemates. The twentieth-century defences – an important element in the castle's history – will also be preserved.

Hurst Castle's exposed position on the narrow shingle spit also means that large sums of money have to be spent attempting to stabilise the shingle with groynes and boulders. Comparing the 1954 aerial photograph on page 15 with the present state of the spit shows the extent of erosion of the seaward side since then. This is probably the result of dredging for gravel.

Appendix: The Armament of Hurst Castle

To be effective as a fortress, Hurst Castle had to have strong armament, good stocks of ammunition and a well-trained garrison. Although records are incomplete, it seems likely that at no stage in its history has the castle had the full quota of weapons designed for it, with the exception of the 1914–18 and 1939–45 wars when batteries of quick-firing guns were deemed adequate. Even when records show weapons installed, their usefulness must be suspect, especially before the nineteenth century. For example, a 1793 report mentions that 'guns might be fired . . . if there were any serviceable to be put upon the seven good carriages that are now there . . . .' Other unknown influences to be considered were the efficiency of the garrison – peacetime 'caretaker' garrisons in the eighteenth century were often composed of the elderly and unfit – and the state of the gunpowder which needed careful storage if it was to maintain its destructive power. All these variables should be borne in mind when assessing the castle's strength in the light of the following weapon lists of random dates.

1547

Although completed in 1544 with embrasures for over 70 weapons of varying calibre, the 1547 survey shows how far practice was short of intent:

1 brass saker, 1 brass demi-culverin, 1 brass culverin, 1 brass demi-cannon, 1 brass curtall cannon, 2 cast-iron demi-culverins, 1 cast-iron saker, 6 cast-iron portpieces, 1 iron sling, 3 iron slings with broken chambers, 2 iron quarter slings and 7 iron bases.

1800

By this date, the castle needed modernising and strengthening if it was to carry the heavier weapons then being favoured for coastal defence. A Board of Ordnance report mentions that the 18 gun platforms in the castle were all in good repair. These were armed with an unstated number of captured French 9 pdr guns. On either side of the castle were two five-gun batteries armed with 36 pdr guns, but 6 of the gun carriages were unserviceable and one was in a poor state.

1905

By then, the heavy RML guns installed in the 1870s were obsolete but most remained in the castle until the end of the 1914-18 war as reserve armament:

Three 12 pdr quick-firing guns
Three 6 pdr quick-firing guns
Ten 12.5-inch RML guns
Fifteen 10-inch RML guns
Four 0.303 machine guns

1941

In the Second World War, Hurst Castle's main task was to guard against surface raiders and aircraft and to watch for submarines. It was part of a formidable defence system protecting the Southampton–Portsmouth area. The castle mounted.

Two 12 pdr quick-firing guns
Two twin 6 pdr quick-firing guns

In July 1943 a Bofors anti-aircraft gun was mounted on the east wing; in January 1944 a second Bofors was mounted on the end of the west wing.

At the beginning of this century, Defence Electric Lights – later abbreviated to Searchlights – were installed at the castle to aid the defence after dark. Searchlights remained part of the castle's equipment until 1956. Their mountings can be seen on the west wing. They were powered by generators installed in the casemates below.

Further reading

COAD, J G (1985) Hurst Castle: The Evolution of a Tudor Fortress 1790–1945, *Post-Medieval Archaeology* 19:63–104

COLVIN, H M *et al* (1982) *The History of the King's Works*, volume 4, London: HMSO

CRASTER, O E (1949) *Hurst Castle*, London: HMSO

KENYON, J R (1979) An aspect of the 1599 survey of the Isle of Wight: The State of all the Queens Ma[ties] Fortresses and Castelles, *Post-Medieval Archaelogy* 13: 61–77

SAUNDERS, A D (1966) Coastal defences since the introduction of artillery, *Archaeological Journal* 123: 136–71

Documentary sources

The Public Record Office, Kew, has a number of early maps and plans of Hurst Castle. Records relating to building and modifying Hurst are also in the WO/44 and WO/55 series. The library of the Royal Engineers, Brompton, Kent, contains a series of letter books (POR/01/–) for the Portsmouth area which contain details of the castle.